"This is a magnificent achievement and so very needed."
  Derek W. H. Thomas, Minister of Preaching and Teaching,
  First Presbyterian Church, Columbia, South Carolina;
  Professor of Systematic Theology and Historical Theology,
  Reformed Theological Seminary

"I appreciate Whitney's contribution to this important area, and it is
my prayer that God will use this widely to strengthen families in the
area of home worship."
  Daniel L. Akin, President, Southeastern Baptist Theological
  Seminary

D0498820

FAMILY WORSHIP

DONALD S. WHITNEY

CROSSWAY®

WHEATON, ILLINOIS

Family Worship

Copyright © 2016 by Donald S. Whitney

Published by Crossway
       1300 Crescent Street
       Wheaton, Illinois 60187

Cover design: Tim Green, Faceout Studio

First printing 2016

Printed in the United States of America

Unless otherwise indicated, all Scripture quotations are from the ESV® Bible (The Holy Bible, English Standard Version®), copyright © 2001 by Crossway. Used by permission. All rights reserved.

Scripture quotations marked NASB are from *The New American Standard Bible*®. Copyright © The Lockman Foundation 1960, 1962, 1963, 1968, 1971, 1972, 1973, 1975, 1977, 1995. Used by permission.

All emphases in Scripture quotations have been added by the author.

Trade paperback ISBN: 978-1-4335-4780-5
ePub ISBN: 978-1-4335-4783-6
PDF ISBN: 978-1-4335-4781-2
Mobipocket ISBN: 978-1-4335-4782-9

Library of Congress Cataloging-in-Publication Data
Whitney, Donald S. (Professor)
  Family worship / Donald S. Whitney.
    pages cm
  Includes bibliographical references and index.
  ISBN 978-1-4335-4780-5 (tp)
  1. Families—Religious life. 2. Worship. I. Title.
BV200.W45   2016
249—dc23   2015026261

Crossway is a publishing ministry of Good News Publishers.

VP		24	23	22	21	20	19	18	17	16
15	14	13	12	11	10	9	8	7	6	5	4	3

Contents

For my family—past, present, and future
and
For my spiritual family in Christ—local and universal

Introduction

Some time ago, I was in England and heard a report on BBC radio about a government study there which indicated that as a result of TV, technology, and the like, families rarely spend time together. The study observed that conversation between family members has "degenerated into an indistinguishable series of monosyllabic grunts." And what was the recommended solution to this dilemma? The government should teach a series of classes instructing families how to talk and play together.

I immediately thought of at least two responses to this report. First, things are *really* bad when the *government* believes that the family is in trouble. Second, God has a much better plan for family time together than anything presented in classes taught by the government.

I had gone to England to speak at a conference. Around the table there one evening, I heard the story of a minister's family who had not acted as though God has a better plan until it was too late. The minister's widow told me that the greatest regret of her life was that her late husband had not begun leading their family in the daily worship of God together until after he was diagnosed with terminal cancer.

Contrast that with a story sent to me by a friend describing what he and his four siblings said at their parents' fiftieth wedding anniversary celebration. He wrote,

> All five of us children decided to express thanks to our father and mother for one thing without consulting each other. Remarkably, all five of us thanked our mother for her prayers and all five of us thanked our father for his leadership of . . . family worship. My brother said, "Dad, the oldest memory I have is of tears streaming over your face as you taught us from *Pilgrim's Progress* on Sunday evenings how the Holy Spirit leads believers. [When I was only] three, God used you in family worship to convict me that Christianity was real. No matter how far I went astray in later years [though today he's an elder in his church], I could never seriously question the reality of Christianity and I want to thank you for that."[1]

Various studies, as well as our own experiences in local church ministry, bear witness to the reality that a high percentage of churchgoing teenagers leave the church once they finish high school. One of the leading problems with this issue is that, unlike the siblings at the fiftieth wedding anniversary celebration, most of these young people have no early, sweet memories of family worship. Such recollections, if they had them, might help prevent their departure from the faith in the first place. Or if they do walk away, the memories might be the means to turn their hearts to seek God again later.

The great British Baptist preacher of the 1800s Charles Spurgeon spoke to this issue, saying,

> Brethren, I wish it were more common, I wish it were universal, with all [Christians] to have family prayer. We sometimes hear of children of Christian parents who do not grow up in the fear of God, and we are asked how it is that they turn out so badly. In many, very many cases, I fear there is such a neglect of family worship that it's not probable that the children are at all impressed by any piety supposed to be possessed by their parents.[2]

I am persuaded from my own ministry experience in hundreds of churches that so little family worship regularly exists in Christian homes today, that even in *most* of our *best* churches, *most* of our *best* men do not even pray with their wives (and children if they have them) much less lead them in ten minutes or so of worship as a family.

A survey by the Barna Research Group supports that claim. According to this report,

> Eighty-five percent of parents with children under age 13 believe they have primary responsibility for teaching their children about religious beliefs and spiritual matters. However, a majority of parents don't spend any time during a typical week discussing religious matters or studying religious materials with their children. . . .

Parents generally rely upon their church to do all of the religious training their children will receive.[3]

Having your family in a Christ-exalting, gospel-centered, Bible-teaching local church is crucial to Christian parenting. But it is not enough for conveying to *your* family all you want to teach them about God and *your* beliefs. Moreover, it is unlikely that exposure to the church once or twice a week will impress your children enough with the greatness and glory of God that they will want to pursue him once they leave your home.

This is why family worship is so important. But even more importantly, God *deserves* to be worshiped daily in our homes by our families.[4]

1

As for Me and My House, We Will Serve the Lord

FAMILY WORSHIP IN THE BIBLE

While there is no direct, explicit commandment in Scripture about family worship, the Bible clearly implies that God deserves to be worshiped daily in our homes by our families. Also, its practice is evident throughout the Bible. To quote Charles Spurgeon,

> I trust there are none here present, who profess to be followers of Christ who do not also practice prayer in their families. We may have no positive commandment for it, but we believe that it is so much in accord with the genius and spirit of the gospel, and that it is

so commended by the example of the saints, that the neglect thereof is a strange inconsistency.[1]

Abraham

Evidence for the practice exists as far back as Genesis 18:17–19 where the Lord and two angels appeared to Abraham in the form of dusty travelers. Abraham provided hospitality for them, and in the course of the conversation it began to dawn upon Abraham who his guests were, especially when one of them said that Sarah would soon find herself expecting the child promised by the Lord to the old, barren couple years before. As the three were leaving and heading toward Sodom and Gomorrah (which the Lord was about to destroy) the Lord spoke:

> Shall I hide from Abraham what I am about to do, seeing that Abraham shall surely become a great and mighty nation, and all the nations of the earth shall be blessed in him? *For I have chosen him, that he may command his children and his household after him to keep the way of the LORD* by doing righteousness and justice, so that the LORD may bring to Abraham what he has promised him.

We have no reason to believe that much true worship of the true God existed in Abraham's day. In fact, after the Tower of Babel episode in Genesis 11 when the Lord confused the languages of people and scattered them, it is difficult to identify anyone else in the world at that point in the Bible, outside of Abraham's family, who loved the true God.[2] But as the Lord did centuries earlier with Noah, God graciously chose to reveal himself to Abraham. And he did so in part, we are told, "that [Abraham] may command his children and his household after him to keep the way of the LORD."

When would Abraham have done this? He did not have others to rely upon. He could not turn for help, as we can, to the ministries of a local church. The only way Abraham could have commanded his children to keep the way of the Lord was to teach the things of God at home.

Once Abraham and Sarah's miracle baby Isaac arrived, Abraham obviously did more than merely provide a good home education about keeping the way of the Lord. Abraham obviously led Isaac and the rest of his family in the *worship* of God.

This is plainly implied in the story of Abraham and Isaac in Genesis 22. God tested Abraham by telling him to offer up Isaac as a sacrifice. Early the next morning, the old man obeyed by getting everything together—even splitting the wood himself—and heading for Mount Moriah. There he intended to sacrifice his only son to God because of his faith in God and his confidence that God could raise Isaac from the dead (Heb. 11:17–19).

Those familiar with the story will know that the Lord intervened at the last moment and provided a ram to be sacrificed as a substitute for Isaac. But in Genesis 22:6–7, Abraham did not yet know that Lord would speak and spare him the agony of killing Isaac. The key element of this story in support of family worship actually happens before that dramatic climax. Isaac knew they were going to the mountain to offer a sacrifice and worship God (though not yet aware that the plan was for him to be the sacrifice). Abraham and Isaac had traveled for two days and had reached the foot of Mount Moriah. As they prepared for the final leg of their journey, we read that:

> Abraham took the wood of the burnt offering and laid it on Isaac his son. And he took in his hand the fire and the knife. So they went both of them together. And Isaac said to his father Abraham, "My father!" And he said, "Here I am, my son." He said, "Behold, the fire and the wood, but where is the lamb for a burnt offering?" (Gen. 22:6–7)

How did Isaac know that they did not have everything necessary for a sacrifice? How did he know that the worship of God involved fire, wood, and a lamb? Or that the lamb would be sacrificed as a burnt offering? Isaac knew these things because he must have long been familiar with sacrifices and the worship of God. Isaac must have often seen the wood split and piled for a sacrifice. He must have heard the crackle of the fire and smelled the burning flesh of a lamb offered to God before. Therefore, Isaac knew when an element of the worship of God was missing because Abraham must have frequently led his family in the worship of God.

Moses

Perhaps the best-known text in the Bible commanding families to teach their children is found in the words of Moses in Deuteronomy 6:4–7:

> Hear, O Israel: The LORD our God, the LORD is one. You shall love the LORD your God with all your heart

and with all your soul and with all your might. And these words that I command you today shall be on your heart. You shall teach them diligently to your children, and shall talk of them when you sit in your house, and when you walk by the way, and when you lie down, and when you rise.

There is much more here than family worship. But family worship can comprise an integral part of obedience to this command. Parents should teach the things of God to their children at every opportunity, as the verse says, and they should do so with their children, individually and collectively. But both in biblical times and today, the best time for parents to teach the things of God to their children on a *consistent* basis when *all* their children are present would be during a time of family worship.

Joshua

Have you ever considered how infrequently people gathered for congregational worship in the centuries comprising nearly the entire Old Testament? Even after the tabernacle and temple were built believers did not gather in large groups to worship God as often as is sometimes assumed. Only after the Babylonian exile, late in Old Testament history and hundreds of years after Solomon built the temple, did the local synagogues develop and people begin to worship God congregationally on a weekly basis. Of course, with the coming of Jesus and the outpouring of the Holy Spirit, most believers are now privileged to experience the riches of being in God's family through regular participation in a local church.

But God was as worthy of worship in the days before regular congregational worship as he is now. Those who believed in and loved God, people such as Abraham, Isaac, Jacob, Joseph, Moses, Joshua, and others, wanted to worship God in their days as much as his people do today. Keep that thought in mind as you read the famous words of Joshua 24. This great successor of Moses had led God's people into the Promised Land and been their leader for decades. Near the end of his life, he once more exhorted the Israelites to remain faithful to God. In Joshua 24:15 he declared,

> And if it is evil in your eyes to serve the LORD, choose this day whom you will serve, whether the gods your fathers served in the region beyond the River, or the gods of the Amorites in whose land you dwell. But as for me and my house, we will serve the LORD.

How would Joshua and his house have served the Lord? Part of serving the Lord for them back then, just as it is for us now, is worshiping the Lord. But in a day when congregational worship was so infrequent—after all, for many Israelites it involved a trip of several days to travel to the tabernacle—regular family worship of some sort would have been a part of carrying out Joshua's resolve, "as for me and my house, we will serve the LORD."

Job

The book of Job begins with a description of his devotion to God, the size of his family, and the abundance of his wealth.

Verse 4 of chapter one tells how Job's seven sons would take turns hosting feasts, events at which they would also invite their three sisters. After each feast, verse 5 explains,

> When the days of the feast had run their course, Job would send and consecrate them [that is, his sons and daughters], and he would rise early in the morning and offer burnt offerings according to the number of them all. For Job said, "It may be that my children have sinned, and cursed God in their hearts." Thus Job did continually.

So whenever one of his sons had such a feast, afterward Job would send for his children, and when they were all together he would get up early the next morning and lead his family in the worship of God by offering sacrifices to the Lord on their behalf.

Asaph

In Psalm 78:1–8 we read the inspired words of a psalmist named Asaph. He was one of the three leaders of music appointed by King David in the days of the tabernacle. Asaph wrote,

> Give ear, O my people, to my teaching;
>   incline your ears to the words of my mouth!
> I will open my mouth in a parable;
>   I will utter dark sayings from of old,
> things that we have heard and known,
>   that our fathers have told us.

We will not hide them from their children,
>   *but tell to the coming generation*
the glorious deeds of the LORD, and his might,
>   and the wonders that he has done.

He established a testimony in Jacob
>   and appointed a law in Israel,
which *he commanded our fathers*
>   *to teach to their children,*
that the next generation might know them,
>   *the children yet unborn,*
and arise and tell them to their children,
>   so that they should set their hope in God
and not forget the works of God,
>   but keep his commandments;
and that they should not be like their fathers,
>   a stubborn and rebellious generation,
a generation whose heart was not steadfast,
>   whose spirit was not faithful to God.

God "commanded . . . fathers" among his people (v. 5) to "tell to the coming generation the glorious deeds of the LORD" (v. 4). The term *glorious deeds* is rendered "praises"[3] or "praiseworthy deeds"[4] in most other major translations. Asaph listed several examples of God's "praises" in the rest of Psalm 78, including the miracles he performed in Egypt and during the exodus (vv. 9–53), and the "praiseworthy deeds" he performed after the Israelites arrived in the Promised Land, such as his frequent defeat of their enemies and his shepherding of Israel through his choice of David as king (vv. 54–72).

Sadly, despite the many "glorious deeds" God did for his people, faithfulness to the record also required Asaph to report "how often they rebelled against him" (v. 40).

Here in Psalm 78, God commanded fathers to "tell to the coming generation" (v. 4) these things so they would not follow the rebellious example of previous generations, but instead would "set their hope in God and not forget the works of God, but keep his commandments" (v. 7).

So, when would the fathers first addressed by Asaph have obeyed this command from the Lord? When would the fathers have taught the "glorious deeds" and "praises" of the Lord to their children?

I'm sure you can imagine the fathers in the days of King David telling stories of the Lord's "praiseworthy deeds" to their children gathered around a fire or a meal. But "praises" are also something we teach in worship, similar to when we hear a worship leader at church say, "I'm going to teach a new song today for us to sing in the worship of God."

Would the fathers have taught "the praises of the Lord" in congregational worship? Perhaps sometimes they would. But this passage seems to be speaking more on an intimate and family level (that is, fathers and children) than a congregational one. Besides, as we've already noted, even by the time the psalms were written there was much less congregational worship than we might imagine, and some of this probably involved segregating the fathers from the rest of the family. And even if the family members were all together, they were not inside the tabernacle (which was still in operation at the time of Psalm 78). The tabernacle was smaller than most church buildings in America today and only priests were allowed to enter, so it was a physical impossibility for all the gathered Israelites to be inside it. When all the people in the time of David and Asaph did gather to worship God congregationally—such as at one of the major feasts—everything happened as they stood outside together by the thousands.

So the instruction Asaph spoke of in Psalm 78 almost certainly did not occur in a congregational setting. Rather, fathers taught these "praises" to their children at home. And some of that teaching happened as the fathers led their families in the most regular kind of group worship they could have experienced, family worship.

Paul

Over in the New Testament, married men find these instructions in Ephesians 5:25–26: "Husbands, love your wives, as Christ loved the church and gave himself up for her, that he might sanctify her, having cleansed her by the washing of water with the word." As Christ cleansed his bride, the church, by the washing of the water of the Word of God,[5] so husbands are exhorted here to love their wives in like manner. And one of the best ways that husbands can bring the pure water of the Word of God into their homes is through the spiritually cleansing and refreshing practice of family worship.

Then we read these familiar words in Ephesians 6:4: "Fathers, do not provoke your children to anger, but bring them up in the discipline and instruction of the Lord." If you're a dad, you do not expect others to do this for you, do you? Of course not. God gave this command to you as your direct responsibility. So I ask you, when do you do this?

Besides providing a general Christian worldview for your family, *when*, specifically, do you bring your children up "in the discipline and instruction of the Lord"? Yes, of course you do it when you bring your children to church. Yes, of course you do it when you converse with them about the things of God from time to time at home or in the car. Yes, of course you even do it through your personal example. But bringing children up "in the discipline and instruction of the Lord" does not happen only unintentionally and incidentally.

Yes, it should and does happen at unplanned, teachable moments in the car, at bedtime, and so on throughout the day. That's wonderful! But it should also happen purposefully. And without some regularity, structure, and purpose, bringing our children up "in the discipline and instruction of the Lord" is one of those things that we can assume we are doing but never actually do as well as we might think. Consistent, father-led family worship is one of the best, steadiest, and most easily measurable ways to bring up children in the Lord's "discipline and instruction." Besides bringing your children to church, you can point to those regular times of family worship and say, "That's one of the most important ways we practice—specifically, audibly, and observably—what the Lord commands in Ephesians 6:4."

Did you realize that a proven commitment to family worship is implied as one of the qualifications for being an elder (that is, a pastor)? The apostle Paul writes about these qualifications in 1 Timothy 3. In verses 4–5 he says this about an elder: "He must manage his own household well, with all dignity keeping his children submissive, for if someone does not know how to manage his own household, how will he care for God's church?" In light of this, it is fair to ask, If a man cannot manage worship in his own household, how can he manage worship in the church? If he cannot lead family worship, how can he lead church worship?

Peter

In 1 Peter 3:7, the apostle Peter assumes not only that church elders would practice family worship, but that all Christian husbands would do so: "Likewise, husbands, live with your wives in an understanding way, showing honor to the woman as the weaker vessel, since they are heirs with you of the grace of life, so that your prayers may not be hindered." Have you realized that the prayers here are those prayed *together* by husbands and wives? It is also true that the individual prayers of the husband will be hindered if he does not live with his wife in an understanding way and if he does not show honor to her. The fact that our personal sin affects our personal prayers is made plain in Psalm 66:18, "If I regard wickedness in my heart, the Lord will not hear" (NASB). But here in 1 Peter 3:7 the text speaks of mutual prayer. Peter assumes that Christian couples pray together. He expected Christian husbands to conduct family worship. This is the norm for holy husbanding. Spurgeon said on this verse, "[This] text would be most appropriately used to stimulate Christians to diligence in family prayer. . . . I esteem it so highly that no language of mine can adequately express my sense of its value."[6]

———

The Bible clearly implies that God deserves to be worshiped daily in our homes by our families. The beloved Bible commentator Matthew Henry knew this when he said, "The way of family worship is a good old way, no new thing, but the ancient usage of the saints."[7] That statement is true not only of the saints (that is, the believers) in the Bible but has been true of God's people ever since.

2

Here the Reformation
Must Begin

FAMILY WORSHIP IN CHURCH HISTORY

The lives of our Christian heroes testify that God deserves to be worshiped daily in our homes by our families. For instance, we know that the first generations of Christians consistently worshiped God as families. Lyman Coleman, a scholar of early church history, writes about the family worship practices of the Christians in the decades immediately after New Testament times:

> At an early hour in the morning the family was assembled and a portion of Scripture was read from the

Old Testament, which was followed by a hymn and a prayer, in which thanks were offered up to the Almighty for preserving them during the silent watches of the night, and for His goodness in permitting them to meet in health of body and soundness of mind; and, at the same time, His grace was implored to defend them amid the dangers and temptations of the day,—to make them faithful to every duty, and enable them, in all respects, to walk worthy of their Christian vocation. . . . In the evening, before retiring to rest, the family again assembled, the same form of worship was observed as in the morning, with this difference, that the service was considerably protracted beyond the period which could be conveniently allotted to it in the commencement of the day.[1]

Tertullian

In the second century, a theologian named Tertullian (c. 160–225) wrote about marriage between believers. While no doubt idealizing the relationship, in the midst of his portrayal he describes family worship as an integral part of a Christian home:

They pray together, they worship together, they fast together; instructing one another, encouraging one another, strengthening one another. . . . Psalms and hymns they sing to one another, striving to see which one of them will chant more beautifully the praises of their Lord. Hearing and seeing this, Christ rejoices.[2]

John Chrysostom

Widely considered one of the greatest preachers in the history of the church is the fourth-century archbishop of Constantinople, John Chrysostom (c. 349–407). Historian Philip Schaff says that Chrysostom "urged that every house should be church, and every head of a family a spiritual shepherd, remembering the account he must give even for his children."[3]

Martin Luther

As individual access to the Bible became increasingly rare and expensive, and with the progressively more hierarchical clergy, family worship generally declined into dust from about this point in Christian history until the Reformation. But when the Bible reentered the house, so did family worship. By the time of Martin Luther (1483–1546), the trend began to reverse and the windows of a recovery of family worship were thrown open. Luther preached almost every day, pastored a church, and wrote massive amounts of theology and Bible commentary. But he also recognized that like any other Christian husband and father, he had the responsibility to be the worship-leading pastor of his family. In one place Luther wrote of

> Abraham [who] had in his tent a house of God and a church, just as today any godly and pious head of a household instructs his children . . . in godliness. Therefore such a house is actually a school and church, and the head of the household is a bishop and priest in his house.[4]

John Knox

Half a generation later in the 1500s, John Knox (1514–1572) led the Reformation into Scotland. This is the man of God of whom the Roman Catholic Mary, Queen of Scots, reportedly said, "I fear the prayers of John Knox more than all the assembled armies of Europe." In a letter to his Christian brothers in Scotland in 1556, Knox said this about family worship: "Brethren, ye are ordained of God to rule your own houses in his true fear, and according to his word. . . . And therefore, I say, ye must make them partakers in reading, exhorting, and in making common prayers, which I would in every house were used once a day at least."[5]

The Westminster Confession of Faith and
the Second London Confession of 1689

In the next century, both the Presbyterians and the Baptists considered family worship so important that they included statements about it in their confessions of faith.[6] In the most influential Presbyterian doctrinal statement ever—the Westminster Confession of Faith—and the most influential Baptist confession of faith ever—the Second London Confession of 1689—documents still adopted by thousands of churches around the world, the practice of family worship is explicitly prescribed. In both documents, we read this: "God is to be worshipped everywhere in spirit and in truth; *as in private families daily*, and in secret each one by himself."[7]

The Westminster Assembly completed its work on the Confession in 1647. In August of that year the Church of

Scotland, still carrying forward the vision of John Knox, thought family worship so important that it created a companion document to the Westminster Confession called *The Directory for Family Worship*. This guide contains fourteen divisions, including sections on the reason for family worship, the proper use of Scripture in it, the responsibility of the husband and father to lead family worship, directions for family prayer, and more.

But the directory was not just a collection of suggestions for the exceptionally devoted men in the church. In the preamble, the church elders were required to keep the heads of the households accountable to their God-given responsibility for family worship. If they failed, they were to be admonished privately. And for any husband or father who continued to neglect his spiritual responsibility to his family, *The Directory for Family Worship* gave these instructions:

> He is to be gravely and sadly reproved by the session [that is, the elders]; after which reproof, if he be found still to neglect Family-worship, let him be, for his obstinacy in such an offence, suspended and debarred from the Lord's supper, as being justly esteemed unworthy to communicate therein, till he amend.[8]

In other words, these Christian leaders from across Scotland and the thousands of Presbyterian churches throughout Great Britain and abroad that would soon come to adopt this document thought family worship so essential for the spiritual health of their families, and so indispensable for the souls of their children, that any man who dared abandon his family spiritually in this way was to receive church discipline.

The English Puritans

In his classic work, *The Worship of the English Puritans*, Horton Davies writes of "the high esteem in which Family Worship was held by the Puritans."[9] Consistent with *The Directory of Family Worship*, the Puritans, according to J. I. Packer, believed "it was the husband's responsibility to channel the family into religion, . . . to lead the family in worship daily, ideally twice a day; and to set an example of sober godliness at all times and in all matters. To this end he must be willing to take time out to learn the faith that he is charged to teach."[10]

Richard Baxter

Pastor Richard Baxter (1615–1651) epitomized the Puritan position by teaching that, "Solemn prayer and praises of God in and by Christian families is of divine appointment. . . . Family prayer and praises are a duty owned by the teaching and sanctifying work of the Spirit; therefore they are of God."[11]

Then Baxter threw down this challenge:

> I willingly appeal to the experience of all the holy families in the world. Who ever used these duties seriously, and found not the benefits? What families be they, in which grace and heavenly-mindedness prosper, but those that use these duties? Compare in all your towns, cities, and villages, the families that read the Scriptures, pray, and praise God, with those that do not, and see

the difference; which of them abound more with impiety, with oaths, and cursings, and railings, and drunkenness, and whoredoms, and worldliness, and such; and which abound most with faith, and patience, and temperance, and charity, and repentance, and hope, and such. The controversy is not hard to decide.[12]

Matthew Henry

A man born fifty years after Baxter, but who became just as well known to the church around the world for his commentary on the Bible, is Matthew Henry (1662–1714). His biographer wrote,

> Matthew's conduct in his family . . . was in a great measure regulated by the example of his pious father, of whose house those who had access to it were ready to say, *This is no other than the house of God, and the gate of heaven.* Matthew was constant in the worship of God in his family, morning and evening, which nothing was suffered to prevent. . . . He was never tedious, but always full and comprehensive, performing much in a little time. . . . When the whole was ended, his children came to him for his blessing, which he gave with solemnity and affection.[13]

Matthew Henry himself wrote, "Turn your families into little churches."[14] And,

> If therefore our houses be houses of the Lord, we shall for that reason love home, reckoning our daily devo-

tion the sweetest of our daily delights; and our family-worship the most valuable of our family-comforts. . . . A church in the house will be a good legacy, nay, it will be a good inheritance, to be left to your children after you.[15]

And it was Matthew Henry who made one of the most remarkable of all statements on this subject. Regarding family worship he said, "Here the reformation must begin."[16] In other words, the reformation that we long for and pray for in our churches also involves the home. Since the church is comprised of family units—from singles to large families and everything in between—if the homes are changed through family worship, the church will be changed.

Jonathan Edwards

The great Jonathan Edwards (1703–1758) is known for his intellectual abilities, his devotional passion, his powerful preaching, and his insightful writing. But we should also remember him for the consistent Christian family life that he and his godly wife, Sarah, modeled, and for the influence this had on their eleven remarkable children. Edwards, according to biographer George Marsden,

Began the day with private prayers followed by family prayers, by candlelight in winter.[17]

Care for his children's souls was, of course, his preeminent concern. In morning devotions he quizzed them on Scripture with questions appropriate to their ages.[18]

Each meal was accompanied by household devotions, and at the end of each day Sarah joined him in his study for prayers.[19]

Samuel Davies

Samuel Davies (1724–1761), the man who succeeded Jonathan Edwards as president of Princeton and described by no less than Martyn Lloyd-Jones as one of America's greatest preachers, said of family worship:

> If you love your children; if you would bring down the blessing of heaven upon your families: if you would have your children make their houses the receptacles of religion when they set up in life for themselves; if you would have religion survive in this place, and be conveyed from age to age; if you would deliver your own souls—I beseech, I entreat, I charge you to begin and continue the worship of God in your families from this day to the close of your lives. . . . Consider family religion not merely as a duty imposed by authority, but as your greatest privilege granted by divine grace.[20]

J. W. Alexander

J. W. Alexander (1804–1859) was a godly and influential Presbyterian minister in New York in the first half of the nineteenth century. His book, *Thoughts on Family Worship*,[21] is one the best treatments on the subject available. In the preface, he is astonished that "there are many heads of families, communicants in our churches, and, according to a scarcely credible report, some ruling elders and deacons who maintain no stated daily service of God [that is, family worship] in their dwellings."

In the brief chapters of his book, Pastor Alexander deals tenderly, winsomely, and practically with subjects like "The Influence of Family Worship on Individual Piety . . . on Parents . . . [and] on Children." He writes about "Family Worship as a Means of Intellectual Improvement," especially in learning the Bible. He writes persuasively about "The Influence of Family Worship on Domestic Harmony and Love . . . on a Household in Affliction . . . on Visitors, Guests, and Neighbors . . . [and] on Perpetuating Sound Doctrine." I think he is most compelling when addressing the "The Influence of Family Worship on the Church" and "The Influence of Family Worship on Posterity." But in his concluding chapter he says bluntly, "Laying aside all flattering words, I may say plainly that I regard the neglect of family worship as springing from lukewarmness and worldliness in religion."[22]

But, that's not true if people have never learned about family worship. You can't expect Christians to do what they've never been taught to do. I once taught a class of 115 seminary students, in which I asked, "How many of you grew up in homes where family worship was practiced?" Only *seven* raised their hands. Then I asked, "How many have visited in homes where you have seen family worship taking place?" *No one* raised a hand. In a conservative, Bible-believing seminary which attracts some of the most devoted, gospel-zealous Christians on the planet, people preparing to be pastors and missionaries, only one out of sixteen students in a class on spirituality had any familiarity whatsoever with family worship.

What does that say about the situation regarding family worship in our churches, the kinds of churches that are blessed to produce such committed young believers? What is the likelihood that the seminary students who have never even seen family worship would go into the ministry and teach people to practice it and how to do so? Of course, if they were not first taught about family worship themselves, we would never imagine them teaching it to others.

So we can't agree with Alexander that "the neglect of family worship [springs] from lukewarmness and worldliness in religion" if people have never heard of it. But, in reading this book, now *you* have.

Charles Spurgeon

The prince of preachers, Charles Spurgeon (1834–1892), spoke often about family worship. In one place he said,

> If we want to bring up a godly family, who shall be a seed to serve God when our heads are under the clods of the valley, let us seek to train them up in the fear of God by meeting together as a family for worship.[23]

Spurgeon practiced what he preached.[24] After his death, his wife Susannah wrote this glimpse into their lives together with their twin boys, both of whom became pastors:

> After the meal was over, an adjournment was made to the study for family worship, and it was at these seasons that my beloved's prayers were remarkable for their tender childlikeness, their spiritual pathos, and

their intense devotion. He seemed to come as near to God as a little child to a loving father, and we were often moved to tears as he talked thus face to face with his Lord.[25]

A visitor to the Spurgeon home once wrote,

One of the most helpful hours of my visits to Westwood was the hour of family prayer. At six o'clock all the household gathered into the study for worship. Usually Mr. Spurgeon would himself lead the devotions. The portion read was invariably accompanied with exposition. How amazingly helpful those homely and gracious comments were. I remember, especially, his reading of the twenty-fourth of Luke: "Jesus Himself drew near and went with them." How sweetly he talked upon having Jesus with us wherever we go. Not only to have Him draw near at special seasons, but to go with us whatever labour we undertake. . . . Then, how full of tender pleading, of serene confidence in God, of world-embracing sympathy were his prayers. . . . His public prayers were an inspiration and benediction, but his prayers with the family were to me more wonderful still. . . . Mr. Spurgeon, when bowed before God in family prayer, appeared a grander man even than when holding thousands spellbound by his oratory.[26]

John G. Paton

John G. Paton (1824–1907) was a missionary to cannibals in the New Hebrides islands of the South Pacific in the last half of the nineteenth century. Once when writing about his father, he noted how as a young man he appealed to his father (John's grandfather) to maintain family worship every day of the week and not just on Sunday. The result was that as a teenager, he himself often led the daily gathering of his parents and siblings in worship. "And so began," writes John Paton of his father,

> in his seventeenth year that blessed custom of Family Prayer, morning and evening, which my father prac-ticed probably without one single avoidable omission till he lay on his deathbed, seventy-seven years of age; when, even to the last day of his life, a portion of Scrip-ture was read, and his voice was heard softly joining in the Psalm, and his lips breathed the morning and evening Prayer,—falling in sweet benediction on the heads of all his children, far away many of them over all the earth, but all meeting him there at the Throne of Grace. None of us can remember that any day ever passed unhallowed thus; no hurry for market, no rush to business, no arrival of friends or guests, no trouble or sorrow, no joy or excitement, ever prevented at least our kneeling around the family altar, while the High Priest led our prayers to God, and offered himself and his children there. And blessed to others, as well as to ourselves, was the light of such example! I have heard that in long after-years, the worst woman in the village, . . . then leading an immoral life, but since changed by the grace of God, was known to declare, that the only thing that kept her from despair and from the Hell of

the suicide, was when in the dark winter nights she crept close up underneath my father's window, and heard him pleading in Family Worship that God would convert "the sinner from the error of wicked ways, and polish him as a jewel for the Redeemer's crown." "I felt," said she, "that I was a burden on that good man's heart, and I knew that God would not disappoint *him*. That thought kept me out of Hell, and at last led me to the only Saviour."[27]

Martyn Lloyd-Jones

One of the most influential preachers of the twentieth century was Martyn Lloyd-Jones (1899–1981) of London. Iain Murray, his assistant pastor for a while and later Lloyd-Jones's biographer, wrote that family worship was an essential part of his Christianity. "Family prayer," Murray wrote of Lloyd-Jones, "marked the close of every day, and after his death Bethan Lloyd-Jones was to say that it was here that she experienced her greatest loss."[28]

Erroll Hulse

A friend of Lloyd-Jones was the British Baptist leader, Erroll Hulse (b. 1931), who wrote:

Of foremost importance is family worship. That practice is something we must maintain at all costs. Tremendous and relentless pressures come upon families as far as time and commitments are concerned. What we used to call the family altar, the habit of daily family devotions and prayers, is the first to suffer. We ought to read the Scriptures and pray together as families every day.[29]

Don Carson

Twenty-first-century believers also affirm family worship, men such as New Testament scholar Don Carson (b. 1946) who said,

> Like most couples, we have found that sustained time for prayer together is not easy to maintain. Not only do we live at a hectic pace, but each stage of life has its peculiar pressures. When you have two or three pre-school-age children, for instance, you are up early and exhausted by evening. Still, we have tried to follow a set pattern. Quite apart from grace at meals, . . . and quite apart from individual times for prayer and Bible reading, as a family we daily seek God's face.[30]

John Piper

Internationally known pastor and author, John Piper (b. 1946), has likewise emphasized the imperative of a man's fundamental commitment to family worship: "You have to decide how important you think these family moments are. It is possible— for little ones and teenagers and parents. You may have to work at it. But it can be done."[31]

———

We could summarize the views of our Christian heroes across the centuries with a sentence from Jonathan Edwards: "Every

Christian family ought to be as it were a little church."[32] And part of the life of that little church, of course, would include family worship.

How, then, should we practice family worship? What does family worship look like in real life?

Read, Pray, and Sing

THE ELEMENTS OF FAMILY WORSHIP

Basically, there are three elements to family worship: read the Bible, pray, and sing. Only three syllables to remember—read, pray, sing. Jerry Marcellino, in his useful booklet, *Recovering the Lost Treasure of Family Worship*[1] uses three *S*'s as a reminder: Scripture, supplication, and song. But the elements are so simple that you probably will not need any reminders about what to do. And you don't need to prepare anything beforehand. Just read, pray, and sing.

Just Read, Pray, and Sing

Read the Bible

Chapter by chapter, read through books of the Bible together. The younger the children, the more you will want to use narrative passages and read shorter sections.[2] As the children get older, set a goal to read through the entire the New Testament, and later through the entire Bible.

Read enthusiastically and interpretively. In other words, don't be one of those people who reads the Bible as apathetically as if reading a phone directory out loud. It is the Word of God—read it to the best of your ability.

Also, explain any words the children may not understand. Clarify the meaning of key verses. To improve their understanding, perhaps ask the children to choose a verse or phrase to explain to you, and then have them pick one for you to explain to them.

Pray

Whether prayer is offered by the father only, or by someone he designates, or by each member of the family in turn, be sure to pray together. Some people keep a prayer list. Some simply ask for prayer requests from the family. Whatever your approach, pray about at least one thing suggested to you and your family by the Scripture passage you have read.[3]

Some families, regardless of where they were reading in the Bible, always go to the book of Psalms when it's time to pray and turn the words of a few verses there into a prayer. If praying through Psalm 23, for instance, after reading the first verse you might thank the Lord for being your Shepherd, ask him to shepherd your family through certain events or decisions, and so forth. As you have time, continue through the passage line by line, speaking to God about what comes to mind while reading the text.

By using this approach you will not only pray for your family (and in fresh and unique ways each time), but you'll also teach them by example how to pray.

Sing

If possible, get songbooks for everyone. Your church may have some unused or older ones closeted away that you could acquire, perhaps at no cost. Your pastor or a worship leader at your church may be able to recommend other songbooks too. The lyrics of many older, public domain (that is, not copyrighted) songs are also available free on the Internet.

Some people sing a different song each time; some sing the same song for a week so they can learn it. As to music, some families sing along with recordings, while others use family musicians. My perception is that most families—even when it's only a husband and wife—simply sing without accompaniment.

Why Read, Pray, and Sing?

Why not just read and pray and omit singing? Or why not read, pray, sing, and also take the Lord's Supper together?

For starters, do you remember Lyman Coleman's account (from chapter 2) of the family worship practices of believers in the decades immediately after the apostles? The earliest record of Christian family worship describes a pattern of reading Scripture, praying together, and singing praise to God.

Second, when you examine a list of the activities the Bible says to do in worship,[4] only three things on that already short list are equally as appropriate in family worship or in private worship as in congregational worship. Those activities are reading the Bible, praying, and singing.

Often scriptural elements of public worship simply cannot be accommodated to private or family worship. Preaching, for example, requires both a preacher and hearers, so it wasn't intended for private worship. And preaching—especially when properly distinguished from teaching—is impractical in most family worship situations, not to mention the fact that the vast majority of Christians would not profess any sense of a divine call to preach that most churches require of its preachers. Likewise, the Lord's Supper, commanded by Jesus for us to "do . . . in remembrance of [him]" (Luke 22:19) was given to the church body, not to individual Christians or families. So the New Testament pattern for the bread and the cup has never been one of Christians serving communion to themselves in private, nor of families keeping the ordinance in the exclusivity of their home. Rather, the Lord's Supper was given to celebrate together with the church family and as an expression of communion with the body of Christ.

So, what should we do in family worship? It's simple: read the Bible, pray together, and sing to the Lord.

I've discovered in teaching this idea that sometimes people presume that they need to prepare some sort of lesson or devotional for family worship. *Not so.* Occasionally you may encounter an article, blog post, sermon illustration, or the like that you want to share with the family as a means of conveying biblical teaching. *Great!* Or from time to time you might relate an insight from your personal devotional experience that was unusually powerful. *Wonderful!* But apart from these exceptions, no preparation for family worship is needed other than someone choosing a song and deciding your method for prayer. Beyond that, just open the Bible to the place where you stopped last time and read, pray, and sing.

Spurgeon concurs that these three things should be the elements of family worship: "I agree with Matthew Henry when he says, 'They that pray in the family do well; they that pray and read the Scriptures do better; but they that pray, and read, and sing do best of all.' There is a completeness in that kind of family worship which is much to be desired."[5]

If Time Permits . . .

After reading, praying, and singing and while the family is still together, if time permits, consider using one or more of the following tools in order to more deliberately bring your children up in "the discipline and instruction of the Lord."

Catechize

Used for centuries by Christians in virtually all traditions, catechizing is a question-and-answer approach to teaching biblical doctrine. I have seen catechisms used successfully with children as young as two years. For example, "Who made you?" is the first question asked in one catechism for very small children. Then the children are taught to answer, "God made me." The questions are reviewed and new ones are learned incrementally so that over time the children absorb a tremendous amount of biblical truth.

Memorizing a good, age-appropriate catechism is as valuable for learning the Bible as memorizing multiplication tables is for learning mathematics. Ask your pastor for recommendations or search for catechisms on the Internet.

Memorize Scripture

The family worship gathering is also a perfect time to review Scripture verses the family members have learned either separately or collectively. If your family participates in a churchwide Scripture memory plan, family worship is the ideal setting for working on the current verse together. Are the children supposed to memorize Scripture for a particular class or program? Check and encourage their progress when gathered for family worship.

If you aren't involved in an organized Bible memory program, consider developing a simple one of your own. Some families do this by working on one or more verses from the book of the Bible they are currently reading. Some work systematically on a long-term project to learn a larger section of Scripture. Others use different plans. Even learning just one verse per month is valuable and takes little extra time.

Read Other Books

Again, time permitting, you might begin your family gathering with some general family reading, after which you enter family worship. Or, at the close of family worship, you might take advantage of the opportunity to read a Christian book or biography to your family.

You're probably aware of studies which demonstrate the many benefits received by the children whose parents read to them. For many families, there's no easier way to ensure a family reading time than by attaching it to another daily event for everyone in the household: family worship.

Three Reminders

Beyond these content-related guidelines, consider these three reminders for your family's daily worship of God:

Brevity

Be brief, otherwise the experience can become tedious. A good average time to read the Bible, pray, and sing is roughly ten minutes, perhaps less if you have very small children. It is usually easy to lengthen the time if the occasion seems to be especially meaningful and family members are asking questions.

Regularity

Try to have a regular time each day for family worship. For some people it works best early in the morning before the family scatters. For others, the most convenient time is at the close of the evening meal. If this is your choice, part of setting the table might include putting the Bible and songbooks close at hand. I would also recommend that you not allow anyone to get up from table until family worship is finished. For once someone says, "Just let me do this first," the others can become impatient or think of things they also need to do, and the sense of family togetherness is lost. A third popular time for family worship is late in the evening or just before bedtime.

Flexibility

Whatever time you choose, consider the wisdom of adapting a time when the family is already accustomed to being together, rather than trying to create another routine gathering during the day. Of course, a set time for family worship each day does not fit the schedule of many families. So if you prefer to enjoy family worship at night but find that your family is often scattered in the evenings, you may have to plan for a morning or noontime gathering—or sometimes adapt family worship to a mobile experience while traveling in your vehicle.

Every family has to flex its worship time occasionally. Just be careful that your flexibility does not lead to inconsistency. Nevertheless, if developing an entirely new family routine is what it takes to begin your family worship, the benefits will be worth whatever it costs.

———

God deserves to be worshiped daily in our homes by our families. This is how you do it. God made it doable. It's simple: just read, pray, and sing. You can do that!

4

No Family Worship
Situation Is Unique

Several specific situations commonly prompt questions about the feasibility of family worship.

What If the Father Is Not a Christian?

The Bible gives no instruction in this case, and Christian moms have responded to this situation in various, good ways. Many have discovered that their unbelieving husbands are quite willing to read the Bible with their families—they only had to be asked. An appeal by the wife, especially when the children join in, with an emphasis on how this will improve family togetherness is sometimes all it takes. Even unbelieving men often sense the need for the family to spend more time together but are unsure of how to make it happen. If the rest of the family develops a solution to a need he himself feels, he may gladly go along. He may have questions about what to do or doubts about whether he can do it, but the wife can resolve these issues in her appeal, explaining that she and the children can help with the praying and singing. And who knows? The Lord may use his Word in family worship to convert the husband.

Of course, many unbelieving husbands will not participate in family worship under any circumstances. In that case, the mother should institute and lead family worship herself, being careful that neither the way nor spirit with which she conducts family worship causes unnecessary offense or turns the children against their father.

What If There Is No Father at Home?

The responsibility to provide "the discipline and instruction of the Lord" (Eph. 6:4) in the home (including family worship) in this case, falls to the mother. If she has a son, she might allow him to have an increasing role in leading family worship, just as John Paton's father often led family worship when he was a teenager. Additionally, she might ask some of the leaders of the church to come by on a regular basis and conduct family worship for her family.

If you are a woman in this situation, remember to ask the Lord to make you a grandmother like Lois or a mother like Eunice. These women were credited by the apostle Paul in 2 Timothy 1:5 with transmitting their faith to Timothy.

Apparently they raised him quite successfully in terms of "the discipline and instruction of the Lord" in their home, for the apostle Paul himself said to Timothy, "from childhood you have been acquainted with the sacred writings, which are able to make you wise for salvation through faith in Christ Jesus" (2 Tim. 3:15).

What If the Children Are Very Young?

In this case, you may need to exercise an extra measure of both discipline and patience. Part of the discipline may be to teach them to stay in a certain place—such as by their mother, or in a particular spot—and to be quiet during the few moments of family worship. Part of the patience required is persevering with the practice of family worship even when the children don't stay in place or remain quiet.

Most children want to play and not to pay attention during family worship, at least not for very long. Since young children cannot concentrate or understand at the same level as older children, families whose children are all quite small should aim for only a very short time of family worship. As much as possible, accommodate what you read and what you sing to their ages. At the very least, in these fast, growing years you will begin to make lasting impressions upon them about the habit and the value of family worship in your home.

So even if you have a child who is fifteen months old and doesn't even know what you are saying, be assured that the child is learning. If we could put his or her infant thoughts into adult language, they might be something like this: *I don't know what it is we do here every night—Dad reads things I don't understand from a big book, then everyone closes their eyes and talks, and after that everyone sings (I like that part)— but whatever it is, it must be important, because we do it every night.* In other words, even when a child cannot grasp the content of what you read, pray, and sing, at the very least the child is beginning to learn that family worship is an important part of the rhythm of your day. Not only that, the child will also grow up believing that family worship is a normal part of life in the home, and as an adult won't need a book like this one to teach him or her about the priority of family worship or how to conduct it. Through discipline and patience, you'll establish a treasured tradition for your family which may continue for generations.

What If There Is a Wide Range of Ages among the Children?

Having children spanning numerous stages of development is often the case and has as many advantages as challenges. In reality, this difficulty involves only one part of family worship—the time in Scripture—for usually most of the family can sing and pray. When you read the Bible together, you will have to make a point to explain and apply things at different levels. You can ask questions suitable to the age of each child (as Jonathan Edwards did). The younger ones may pick up more than you realize when you are teaching the older ones. The older ones can learn from your example how to teach younger ones, so they can do the same in their own families someday.

Some families in this situation conduct family worship twice—once for the older children and once for the younger.

Others alternate the content, one time directing it toward the older ones and aiming it for the younger ones the next time.

Regardless of the challenges to the practice of family worship that exist in large families, take courage, it can be done. How do we know? History teaches us that in recent centuries Christian families were typically larger in number and more diverse in ages than is common today, and yet they were often more faithful in family worship than Christian families are now. So they prove it can be done.

What If There Are No Children at Home?

Remember that 1 Peter 3:7 addresses husbands, not fathers, when it speaks about mutual prayer in the home. Thus family worship is for couples, not just parents. So even though the presence of children in the home intensifies the importance of family worship because it affects the next generation of Christians, the absence of children in the home does not justify the absence of family worship in the home. Youthful newlyweds to senior-citizen empty-nester couples and everyone in between is called to worship God regularly in their home because God is worthy of our daily worship as families.

———

In any case, realize that there is no family worship situation that has not been addressed by Christians for centuries. You are not alone in the circumstances that make family worship difficult, nor are you alone in experiencing its delights. We tend to think that we have unique problems and our flesh wants to excuse us from family worship on the false grounds that our situation is an exception. I've known students who worked night shifts who were married to spouses who had daytime jobs. Even in that difficult situation, they managed to snatch a few moments—almost in passing at the front door— to worship together. Their discipline to worship together surely strengthened their union when so many other things seemed bent on weakening it.

We need to accept the fact that in this sinful world, challenges to family worship arise regularly in *every* home. The blessings of family worship are too dangerous for Satan to let pass unopposed. Nevertheless, we must stand on this bedrock truth: God deserves to be worshiped daily in our homes by our families. And for that reason, *start today.*

5

Isn't This What You Really *Want* to Do?

START TODAY

The worthiness of God to receive your family's worship each day is reason enough to start practicing family worship today. But in addition to that, consider these other good motivations:

- What better way to speak the gospel into your children's lives every day?
- What better way to provide a regular time for your children to learn the things of God from *you*?
- What better way to provide your children with an ongoing opportunity to ask about the things of God in a comfortable context?

- What better way for you to transmit *your* core beliefs to your children?
- What better way for your children to see the ongoing, positive spiritual example of their parents in real life?
- What better way to provide workable, reproducible examples to your children of how to have a distinctively Christian home when they start a home of their own?
- What better way for getting your family together on a daily basis?
- Isn't this what you really *want* to do?

Despite the desire that many men have to begin family worship, some simply lack the resolve. In his *Thoughts on Family Worship*, J. W. Alexander answers eight common objections to starting family worship, but then says that a "single reason operates with more force than all the others put together." It is when a man says—most likely only to himself—"The truth is, I am ashamed to begin."[1]

This happens when a man awakens to his spiritual responsibilities in the home, but because he has failed to lead family worship for so long he feels embarrassed to begin now. Or he fears the sneer of some member of his family when he says he wants to begin daily family worship. Or he is afraid that he is not capable of leading in family worship. Or he is ashamed because, even though he has tried something like this before, he did not stick with it.

For some men their reluctance may be nothing more than the embarrassment of not knowing what to say to their wives and children to get family worship started. Men, all you have to say is something like this: "I have come to believe that the Bible teaches I should be leading us in family worship, and I want to start today. I have a lot to learn about it, but I want to do what I believe God wants me to do. Will you join me?"

Men like Jacob

Husbands, fathers—have the resolve of Jacob in Genesis 35:2–3:

> So Jacob said to his household and to all who were with him, "Put away the foreign gods that are among you and purify yourselves and change your garments. Then let us arise and go up to Bethel, so that I may make there an altar to the God who answers me in the day of my distress and has been with me wherever I have gone."

Like Jacob, stand up with the manly resolve to tell your family that you want to make an altar to God in your home; that is, you want to make your home a place of worship to God. Exhort your family to put away anything (such as TV, the Internet, etc.) that would keep them from worshiping God with you and to arise and follow you as you lead them in worshiping God.

John G. Paton's Father

Let me tell you about a man who had the resolve of Jacob. We are back to the story of missionary John G. Paton and his father (under whose window the immoral woman would come to listen to their family worship). This is the scene of Paton leaving home for the last time, going to the school from which he would then head to the mission field:

> My dear father walked with me the first six miles of the way. His counsels and tears and heavenly conversation on that parting journey are fresh in my heart as if it had been but yesterday; and tears are on my cheeks as freely now as then, whenever memory steals me away to the scene. For the last half-mile or so we walked on together in almost unbroken silence,—my father, as was often his custom, carrying hat in hand, while his long, flowing yellow hair (then yellow, but in later years white as snow) streamed like a girl's down his shoulders. His lips kept moving in silent prayers for me; and his tears fell fast when our eyes met each other in looks for which all speech was vain! We halted on reaching the appointed parting place; he grasped my hand firmly for a minute in silence, and then solemnly and affectionately said:
>
> "God bless you, my son! Your father's God prosper you, and keep you from evil!"
>
> Unable to say more, his lips kept moving in silent prayer; in tears we embraced, and parted. I ran off as fast as I could; and, when about to turn a corner in the road where he would lose sight of me, I looked back and saw him still standing with head uncovered where I had left him—gazing after me. Waving my hat in adieu, I was round the corner and out of sight in an instant. But my heart was too full and sore to carry me further, so I darted into the side of the road and wept for a time.

Then, rising up cautiously, I climbed the dyke to see if he yet stood where I had left him; and just at that moment I caught a glimpse of him climbing the dyke and looking out for me! He did not see me, and after he had gazed eagerly in my direction for a while he got down, set his face towards home, and began to return—his head still uncovered, and his heart, I felt sure, still rising in prayers for me. I watched through blinding tears, till his form faded from my gaze; and then, hastening on my way, vowed deeply and oft, by the help of God, to live and act so as never to grieve or dishonour such a father and mother as He had given me. The appearance of my father, when we parted—his advice, prayers, and tears—the road, the dyke, the climbing up on it and then walking away, head uncovered—have often, often, all through life, risen vividly before my mind, and do so now while I am writing, as if it had been but an hour ago. In my earlier years particularly, when exposed to many temptations, his parting form rose before me as that of a guardian Angel. It is no Pharisaism, but deep gratitude, which makes me here testify that the memory of that scene not only helped, by God's grace, to keep me pure from the prevailing sins, but also stimulated me in all my studies, that I might not fall short of his hopes, and in all my Christian duties, that I might faithfully follow his shining example.[2]

What had led Paton to such a love of his father and his father's example? Paton answers that question:

How much my father's prayers at this time impressed me I can never explain, nor could any stranger understand. When, on his knees and all of us kneeling around him in Family Worship, he poured out his whole soul with tears for the conversion of the Heathen World to the service of Jesus, and for every personal and domestic need, we all felt as if in the presence of the living Saviour, and learned to know and love Him as our Divine Friend. As we rose from our knees, I used to look at the light on my father's face, and wish I were like him in spirit,—hoping that, in answer to his prayers, I might be privileged and prepared to carry the blessed Gospel to some portion of the Heathen World.[3]

Rick Husband

Another man who had the resolve of Jacob was Rick Husband, commander of the Space Shuttle *Columbia* and among the seven astronauts killed on February 1, 2003, when the spacecraft broke apart and disintegrated over Texas just sixteen minutes from their landing in Florida. The day after the tragedy, a memorial service was held for forty-five-year-old Husband and fellow astronaut Mike Anderson at Grace Community Church in Houston where they attended. At that service, a video was played where Husband said,

If I ended up at the end of my life having been an astronaut, but having sacrificed my family along the way or living my life in a way that didn't glorify God, then I would look back on it with great regret. Having become an astronaut would not really have mattered all that much. And I finally came to realize that what really meant the most to me was to try and live my life the way God wanted me to and to try and be a good husband to Evelyn and to be a good father to my children.[4]

But there is much more to Rick Husband's resolve to be a good husband and father than mere words. A week prior to leaving for the flight crew's quarantine, Commander Husband turned to his wife, Evelyn, and said, "I want to make a videotape for Laura and one for Matthew that they can watch each day I'm in orbit. I want the children to know how much I love them and that I'll be thinking about them every day."[5]

At the beginning of the tape he left with his seven-year-old son, Husband said,

Hi, Matthew. I wanted to tell you how much I love you and I wanted to make this tape for you so that you and I could have a devotional time for every day that I'm in space. So, what I am doing is I'm looking at your devotional book and I'm starting on the sixteenth of January, which is our launch day, and what I will do is read through this book and read the Bible verse also and go through the whole thing just like you and I are sitting here on the couch together. I just wanted to do this because I love you so much and I'm going to do one for your sister as well.[6]

How precious do you think those eighteen devotions on video are to that family today? Isn't *this* the kind of legacy you want to leave to your family? Isn't family worship what you really *want* to do?

Be Resolved

Husbands, fathers—if you have been negligent in this duty and great privilege, repent by starting family worship today. Again, you may feel awkward about what to say to your wife or your children about starting, but simply say that God has convicted you of your responsibility to lead in family worship and you want to start at a given time today or tonight. Almost certainly your wife will be thrilled more than you can imagine to hear you say that. Your children may or may not be as enthusiastic, but that does not really matter. The less interest they show, the more your family needs family worship.

The Lord will help you. He does not call his Spirit-begotten sons to this task without giving them the power of the Holy Spirit to accomplish it. The same Father who gave you the gospel and who drew you to Christ will strengthen you by his Spirit to put on this badge of godly manhood.

Family members—have the willing spirit of Jacob's household. After he called them to follow his leadership in the family worship of God, Genesis 35:4 tells us, "So they gave to Jacob all the foreign gods that they had, and the rings that were in their ears. Jacob hid them under the terebinth tree that was near Shechem." Respond just as willingly to the call to family worship in your home. Encourage your husband or dad in his desire to bring the blessing of God upon you. Do not be a stumbling block in his efforts to obey God.

Single men—resolve to begin a time of worship with your

fiancée from the night you become engaged. Build your marriage from the start on the foundation of family worship. This is holy husbanding. And as married men will tell you, it is much easier to begin the worship of God together before your wedding day than after the daily habits and routines of married life have become established. Make family worship a regular part of your life together before you are married and you are much more likely to continue it after you are married.

Single women—resolve not to marry a man who will not pray with you and lead you in worship daily. For if he will not lead you spiritually in this way before you wed, it is very unlikely that he will do so after. If a man shows an interest in marrying you, talk to him about family worship before you commit your life and the lives of your future children to him.[7]

Empty nesters—show your adult children by your newly begun practice of family worship that you can still learn the things of God, and also that you can still repent. Rather than grieving over what you should have done for your children in family worship years ago, begin family worship now and let that be an example not only of your continued growth as a Christian, but also of what your adult children can likewise begin to do. If your children are married, they can immediately learn from and follow your example in their own homes. Be sure to model family worship for them whenever they come to visit.

Remember the Gospel

Let us be clear: faithful involvement in family worship is not the gospel. We are not made right with God by practicing family worship, or by how well we love and provide for our families, or by anything else we do. The gospel—the message that can lead to being right with God—is the truth of what God has done for us through the life, death, resurrection, and ascension of Jesus Christ. The most important way to respond to that message is not engagement in family worship, but first to repent of your sins against God and to believe that Jesus can make you right with God. But blessed is the family where the good news of what God has done through Jesus Christ is declared and discussed, day after day, generation after generation.

Regardless of what anyone else does, let every husband, let every father, let every Christian challenged by these words commit himself to this: "As for me and my house, we will serve the LORD" in family worship (Josh. 24:15).

Discussion Guide

Chapter 1: As for Me and My House, We Will Serve the Lord

Family Worship in the Bible

1. What did you learn in this chapter about the role of family worship in Old Testament times?

2. Which Old Testament passages make the strongest argument for the necessity of family worship?

3. What New Testament texts do you consider most important regarding the necessity of family worship?

4. Can you think of other biblical texts or doctrines that relate to family worship?

5. What are the key Scripture passages which indicate that the responsibility for initiating and conducting family worship lies on the shoulders of the husband/father?

6. Why does the Bible place the responsibility for leading family worship on the husband/father?

Chapter 2: Here the Reformation Must Begin

Family Worship in Church History

1. What impressed you most about the practice of family worship among some of the heroes of church history?

2. Why does the Westminster *Directory for Family Worship* call for church discipline for those men who fail to lead their families in worship?

3. Why would Matthew Henry say of family worship, "Here the reformation must begin"?

4. In the opinion of the author, what is one of the best books ever written on the subject of family worship, and how may families profit from reading it?

5. What are some of the beliefs about family worship that all these Christian heroes apparently held in common?

6. In what ways do you think the practice of family worship was easier in previous centuries than today? Harder? The same?

Chapter 3: Read, Pray, and Sing
The Elements of Family Worship

1. What are the three primary elements of family worship?

2. What suggestions have you found effective for reading the Bible with children?

3. What are some practices to avoid when reading the Bible with children?

4. In addition to the ones found in chapter 3, what are other workable ideas for praying in family worship?

5. In addition to the ones found in chapter 3, what are other workable ideas for singing in family worship?

6. What are some optional elements that families may append to their family worship gathering?

7. What does catechizing in family worship look like? What are some of the benefits of catechizing in family worship?

8. What are some practical tips for families wanting to memorize Scripture together in family worship?

9. What books come to mind as supplemental reading in family worship?

10. On average, how much time would be appropriate for each of the three primary elements of family worship?

11. Why is it important to have a regular time each day for family worship?

12. Why do we need to be both encouraged toward and cautioned against flexibility in the time and duration of family worship?

Chapter 4: No Family Worship Situation Is Unique

But What If . . . ?

1. What are the most important observations to keep in mind in these family worship situations:

- If the father is not a Christian?
- If there is no father at home?
- If the children are very young?
- If there is a wide range of ages among the children?
- If there are no children at home?

2. What other common difficulties with family worship should be discussed?

3. Since so many possible family worship difficulties exist, why are none of them unique?

Chapter 5: Isn't This What You Really *Want* to Do?

Start Today

1. What are some of the practical benefits of family worship?

2. What kinds of things might a man say to his wife and family when he wants to begin the practice of family worship?

3. What kinds of things should *not* be said?

4. What kinds of things might a wife and/or children say to appeal to their husband/father to begin the practice of family worship? What kinds of things should *not* be said?

5. How can the local church help families begin and continue family worship?

6. Why is it important for single adults to make commitments to family worship before they commit themselves to someone in marriage?

7. What is one thing you believe God would have you do now in regard to family worship?

Notes

Introduction
1. Joel Beeke, *Family Worship* (Grand Rapids, MI: Reformation Heritage, 2002), 3.
2. C. H. Spurgeon, "A Pastoral Visit," *Metropolitan Tabernacle Pulpit*, vol. 54 (London: Passmore and Alabaster, 1908; repr., Pasadena, TX: Pilgrim, 1978), 362–63.
3. Barna Research Group (May 6, 2003), quoted in *Current Thoughts and Trends* 19, no. 7 (July 2003), 21. As time increases between this survey and the reading of this book, may we assume that research done today would reveal a statistically significant improvement? Regardless, the most important question is not one about what parents in general do, but whether we ourselves spend "time during a typical week discussing religious matters or studying religious materials" with our families and whether we are among those who "generally rely upon their church to do all of the religious training" of our families.
4. Do not read the word "family" in this book and think only of parents with small children. While the emphasis here is indeed upon families with children living in the home, this includes children of all ages, from newborns to older teens. Moreover, this book is also for those without children in the home, from couples who do not have children to empty nesters. In addition, this book applies to singles in terms of preparation for marriage someday.

Chapter 1: As for Me and My House, We Will Serve the Lord
1. C. H. Spurgeon, "Restraining Prayer," *Metropolitan Tabernacle Pulpit*, vol. 51 (London: Passmore and Alabaster, 1905; repr., Pasadena, TX: Pilgrim, 1978), 327.

2. The lone exception seems to be Melchizedek, that shadowy figure who blessed Abraham and foreshadows Christ in Genesis 14:18–20 (see also Ps. 110:4 and Heb. 5:6, 10; 6:20; 7:1, 10–11, 15, 21).
3. As in the KJV, NASB, NKJV, and HCSB.
4. As in the NIV.
5. As illustrated in his prayer of John 17:17, "Sanctify them in the truth; your word is truth."
6. C. H. Spurgeon, "Hindrances to Prayer," *Metropolitan Tabernacle Pulpit*, vol. 20 (London: Passmore and Alabaster, 1874; repr., Pasadena, TX: Pilgrim, 1981), 506.
7. Matthew Henry, *Matthew Henry's Concise Commentary* (Oak Harbor, WA: Logos Research Systems, 1997), s.v. Genesis 12:6.

Chapter 2: Here the Reformation Must Begin

1. Lyman Coleman, *The Antiquities of the Christian Church* (Andover and New York: Gould, Newman & Saxton, 1841), 376–77.
2. Tertullian, *Ad uxorem* ("To my wife"), bk. 2, ch. 8; available through "The Tertullian Project," accessed December 1, 2014, http://www.tertullian.org/works/ad_uxorem.htm.
3. Philip Schaff, *Nicene and Post-Nicene Christianity: A.D. 311–600,* vol. 3 of *History of the Christian Church* (Grand Rapids, MI: Eerdmans, 1910), 545.
4. Martin Luther, "Lectures on Genesis: Chapters 21–25" in *Luther's Works*, ed. Jaroslav Pelikan (Saint Louis, MO: Concordia, 1964), 384.
5. John Knox, "A Letter of Wholesome Counsel, Addressed to His Brethren in Scotland, 1556," in *The Works of John Knox* (Edinburgh: Banner of Truth, 2014), 4:137.
6. The fact that these groups inserted a statement about family worship in their confessions of faith is especially interesting. Churches usually put their commonly-held *beliefs* in their confessions of faith, and their mutually agreed-upon *activities* (such as commitments to love and pray for one another) in documents known as church covenants. But even though family worship is an activity, these early Presbyterians and Baptists considered the *practice* so essential that they included a declaration about it in their *doctrinal* statements.
7. Section 22.6 in the WCF; 21.6 in the LCF of 1689 (emphasis added).
8. *The Directory for Family Worship*, annotated ed. (Greenville, SC: Greenville Presbyterian Theological Seminary, 1994), 2.
9. Horton Davies, *The Worship of the English Puritans* (Morgan, PA: Soli Deo Gloria, 1997), 278.

10. J. I. Packer, *A Quest for Godliness: The Puritan Vision of the Christian Life* (Wheaton, IL: Crossway, 1990), 270.

11. Richard Baxter, "A Disputation, Whether the Solemn Worship of God in and by Families as Such, Be of Divine Appointment," in *The Practical Works of Richard Baxter, vol. 1: A Christian Directory*, repr. ed. (Ligonier, PA: Soli Deo Gloria, 1990), 415, 417.

12. Ibid.

13. "Memoirs of Matthew Henry, As Written by a Contemporary: S. Palmer," in *Matthew Henry's Commentary on the Whole Bible* (Old Tappan, NJ: Revell, n.d.), 1:vii.

14. *The Complete Works of the Rev. Matthew Henry* (Grand Rapids, MI: Baker, 1979), 1:258.

15. Ibid., 260–61.

16. Ibid., 260.

17. George M. Marsden, *Jonathan Edwards: A Life* (New Haven, CT: Yale University Press, 2003), 133.

18. Ibid., 321.

19. Ibid., 133.

20. "The Necessity and Excellence of Family Religion," in *Sermons of the Reverend Samuel Davies* (Morgan, PA: Soli Deo Gloria, n.d.), 2:86.

21. J. W. Alexander, *Thoughts on Family Worship* (1847; repr. Morgan, PA: Soli Deo Gloria, 1998), v.

22. Ibid., 145.

23. C. H. Spurgeon, "A Pastoral Visit," *Metropolitan Tabernacle Pulpit*, vol. 54 (London: Passmore and Alabaster, 1908; repr., Pasadena, TX: Pilgrim, 1978), 362–63.

24. Some may think Spurgeon lived in a much simpler era that afforded him more time to practice family worship than Christians would have today. I've conducted a great deal of PhD research on Spurgeon's life and pastoral ministry, and can confirm this isn't so. Spurgeon's autobiography, as well as many first-hand observers, tell us that Spurgeon (1) pastored the largest evangelical church in the world at that time (with more than six thousand active members), (2) preached almost every day, (3) edited his sermons for weekly publications, and thereby (4) produced (in the sixty-four volume *Metropolitan Tabernacle Pulpit*) the largest collection of works by any single author in English, (5) wrote an additional one hundred and twenty books (one every four months throughout his entire adult life), (6) presided over sixty-six different ministries (such as the pastors' college he founded), (7) edited a monthly magazine (*The Sword and the Trowel*), (8) typically read five books each week, many of which

he reviewed for his magazine, and (9) wrote with a dip pen five hundred letters per week. God gave Spurgeon an extraordinary capacity for work and productivity. And yet, despite the ceaseless, crushing demands on his schedule, at six each evening, setting aside a to-do list that few could match today, he gathered his wife, twin boys, and all others present in his home at the time for family worship.

25. C. H. Spurgeon, *C. H. Spurgeon's Autobiography*, comp. Susannah Spurgeon and J. W. Harrald (London: Passmore and Alabaster, 1899; repr., Pasadena, TX: Pilgrim, 1992), 64.

26. Arnold Dallimore, *Spurgeon: A New Biography* (Edinburgh: Banner of Truth, 1985), 178–79.

27. John G. Paton, *Missionary to the New Hebrides* (London: Banner of Truth, 1965), 14–15.

28. Iain Murray, *D. Martyn Lloyd-Jones, The Fight of Faith: 1939–1981* (Edinburgh: Banner of Truth, 1990), 763.

29. Erroll Hulse, "The Importance of Family Worship," *Reformation Today*, November–December 1986: 9.

30. D. A. Carson, *A Call to Spiritual Reformation* (Grand Rapids, MI: Baker, 1992), 23.

31. John Piper, *Pierced by the Word* (Sisters, OR: Multnomah, 2003), 73.

32. Jonathan Edwards, *The Complete Works of Jonathan Edwards*, ed. Edward Hickman, 2 vols. (London, 1834; repr., Edinburgh: Banner of Truth, 1974), 1:ccvi.

Chapter 3: Read, Pray, and Sing

1. Jerry Marcellino, *Rediscovering the Lost Treasure of Family Worship* (Laurel, MS: Audubon Press, 1996).

2. With younger children, some prefer to use a Bible-based book designed for a particular age group. Parents who want to use a picture Bible with preschoolers should consider David R. Helm, *The Big Picture Story Bible* (Wheaton, IL: Crossway, 2014) for its consistent gospel emphasis. Those with children ages four to eight will appreciate the Christocentric approach of Sally Lloyd-Jones, *Jesus Storybook Bible: Every Story Whispers His Name* (Grand Rapids, MI: Zonderkidz, 2012). For the same reason, parents of elementary-age children will find Marty Machowski, *Gospel Story Bible: Discovering Jesus in the Old and New Testaments* (Greensboro, NC: New Growth, 2011) a useful option. Since 1935, countless families have used Catherine Vos, *The Child's Story Bible* (Grand Rapids, MI: Eerdmans, 1935) for reading all the narrative passages of the Bible—usually slightly abridged or summarized—to children ages four to ten. A recent addition to biblical narratives written

for children is Kevin DeYoung, *The Biggest Story* (Wheaton, IL: Crossway, 2015).

3. For more on this idea of praying about what you read in the Bible, see Donald S. Whitney, *Praying the Bible* (Wheaton, IL: Crossway, 2015).

4. Such as prayer (Ps. 65:2); the singing of psalms, hymns, and spiritual songs (Col. 3:16; Eph. 5:19); the reading (1 Tim. 4:13) and preaching (2 Tim. 4:2) of Scripture; baptism (Matt. 28:19–20); and the Lord's Supper (1 Cor. 11:23–26).

5. C. H. Spurgeon, "The Happy Duty of Daily Praise," *Metropolitan Tabernacle Pulpit*, vol. 32 (London: Passmore and Alabaster, 1886; repr., Pasadena, TX: Pilgrim, 1986), 289.

Chapter 5: Isn't This What You Really Want to Do?

1. J. W. Alexander, *Thoughts on Family Worship* (1847; repr. Morgan, PA: Soli Deo Gloria, 1998), 151.

2. John G. Paton, *Missionary to the New Hebrides* (London: Banner of Truth, 1965), 25–26.

3. Ibid., 21.

4. "Rick Husband, Mike Anderson 'fervently lived for God,'" *Baptist Press* (blog), February 3, 2003, http://www.bpnews.net/15150.

5. Evelyn Husband with Donna VanLiere, *High Calling* (Nashville: Thomas Nelson, 2003), 2.

6. Ibid., 222.

7. If you are the father of a single woman, and a man shows an interest in marrying your daughter, be sure to speak with him in a timely manner about family worship.

Scripture Index

About the Author

Donald S. Whitney has been professor of biblical spirituality and associate dean at The Southern Baptist Theological Seminary in Louisville, Kentucky, since 2005. Before that he held a similar position at Midwestern Baptist Theological Seminary in Kansas City, Missouri, for ten years. He is the founder and president of The Center for Biblical Spirituality. Don is a frequent speaker in churches, retreats, and conferences in the US and abroad.

Don grew up in Osceola, Arkansas, where he came to believe in Jesus Christ as Lord and Savior. He was active in sports throughout high school and college, and worked in the radio station his dad managed. After graduating from Arkansas State University, Don planned to finish law school and pursue a career in sportscasting. While at the University of Arkansas School of Law, he sensed God's call to preach the gospel of Jesus Christ. He then enrolled at Southwestern Baptist Theological Seminary in Fort Worth, Texas, graduating with a Master of Divinity degree in 1979. In 1987, Don earned a Doctor of Ministry degree at Trinity Evangelical Divinity School in

Deerfield, Illinois. He earned a PhD in theology at the University of the Free State in Bloemfonteine, South Africa, in 2013.

Prior to his ministry as a seminary professor, Don was pastor of Glenfield Baptist Church in Glen Ellyn, Illinois (a Chicago suburb), for almost fifteen years. Altogether he has served local churches in pastoral ministry for twenty-four years.

He is the author of *Spiritual Disciplines for the Christian Life* (NavPress, 1991, 2014), which has a companion discussion guide. He has also written *How Can I Be Sure I'm a Christian?* (NavPress, 1994), *Spiritual Disciplines within the Church* (Moody Press, 1996), *Ten Questions to Diagnose Your Spiritual Health* (NavPress, 2001), *Simplify Your Spiritual Life* (NavPress, 2003), *Finding God in Solitude: The Personal Piety of Jonathan Edwards (1703–1758) and Its Influence on His Pastoral Ministry* (Peter Lang, 2014), and *Praying the Bible* (Crossway, 2015). His hobby is restoring and using old fountain pens.

Don's wife, Caffy, ministers from their home in the Louisville area as a women's Bible study teacher, an artist, and a freelance illustrator. Her website is www.CaffyWhitney.com. The Whitneys have a daughter, Laurelen Christiana.

Don's blog, information about his books, downloadable bulletin inserts, his speaking schedule, subscription information for Don's free e-mail newsletter, and other materials from The Center for Biblical Spirituality are all available at his website, www.BiblicalSpirituality.org. You can find him on Twitter via @DonWhitney and on Facebook.

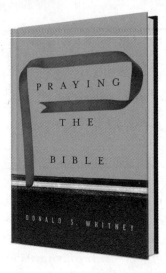

"This little book is explosive and powerful."
R. ALBERT MOHLER JR.

When you pray, does it ever feel like you're just saying *the same old things about the same old things*? Offering us the encouragement and practical advice we're all looking for, Donald S. Whitney outlines an easy-to-grasp method that has the power to transform our prayer life: praying the words of Scripture. Simple yet profound, *Praying the Bible* will prove invaluable as you seek to commune with your heavenly Father in prayer each and every day.

"Whitney offers a wonderfully practical, pastoral, and biblical approach to prayer that relieves personal boredom and unleashes spiritual power."

BRYAN CHAPELL, President Emeritus, Covenant Theological Seminary; Senior Pastor, Grace Presbyterian Church (PCA), Peoria, Illinois

"This is a particularly helpful tool for those of us who often struggle to know what and how to pray or whose minds tend to wander during private prayer."

NANCY LEIGH DEMOSS, author; radio host, *Revive Our Hearts*

For more information, visit crossway.org.